WE CAN DO HARD THINGS

MINDFUL AFFIRMATIONS FOR GREAT KIDS

Written By Jill & Michael Kernsley   Illustrated By Kenneth Oldenburg

We Can Do Hard Things
Copyright © 2021
Smiling Kids Press
smilingkidspress@yahoo.com

Written by Jill and Michael Kernsley
Illustrations by Kenneth Oldenburg
Edited by Gemma White
All Rights Reserved.

Thank you very much for purchasing We Can Do Hard Things!
We wish you and yours all the very best!
For more information please reach out to us at:
thekernsleys@yahoo.com
Yours in Grattitude,
Jill & Michael Kernsley

Please be advised that no part of this book may be reproduced
or used in any manner without written permission of the copyright owners
except for the use of quotations in reviews.

Library of Congress Control Number: 2021909928
ISBN:
978-1-7370801-0-7 Paperback
978-1-7370801-2-1 Hardback

This Book Is Lovingly Dedicated To

_____

A Great Kid, Who's Able To Do Hard Things!

I Always Remember

It's A Win

If I Make A Mistake

I Love To Share

It's Worth It To Do Hard Things

Pick any of the Mindful Affirmations found in We Can Do Hard Things and repeat them slowly.

Say the words out loud or silently to yourself for as little as a few moments or a minute or two.

Imagine experiencing the affirmation and the good energy that's created in both yourself and others.

Even just saying a Mindful Affirmation a couple of times can help build and reinforce positive attitudes that can benefit us in all kinds of different situations.

Dear Friends,

 We thank you so much for purchasing our book. We're very grateful for your support! Because both Michael and I have had benificial results from Postive Affirmations, we truly hope that you and your kids can have similar experiences. Adding in small amounts positive self-talk really makes a wonderful difference!

 Authors Jill and Michael Kernsley share a passion for kids, animals and writing. They both have a desire to make the world a more beautiful and wiser place through their words and actions. They'd love to hear from you at:
      thekernsleys@yahoo.com

 Kenneth Oldenburg is a good hearted, friendly and wonderful artist who has enjoyed drawing since he was a child. With a pen and brush of gold, he loves creating art in a way that children can both feel and take to heart.

CPSIA information can be obtained
at www.ICGtesting.com
Printed in the USA
BVHW022012240621
610384BV00016B/1138